The
Southern
Belle's
Handbook

Also by Loraine Despres

The Scandalous Summer of Sissy LeBlanc

Loraine Despres

The Southern Belle's Handbook

Sissy LeBlanc's
Rules to Live By

WM

William Morrow
An Imprint of HarperCollinsPublishers

HarperCollins books may be purchased for educational, business, or sales promotional use. For information please write: Special Markets Department, HarperCollins Publishers Inc., 10 East 53rd Street, New York, NY 10022.

FIRST EDITION

Design by Shubhani Sarkar
Illustrations by Bethann Thornburgh

Library of Congress Cataloging-in-Publication Data
Despres, Loraine.
　　The southern belle's handbook : Sissy LeBlanc's rules
to live by / Loraine Despres.
　　　　p. cm.
　　ISBN 0-06-054089-3
　　　　1. Man-woman relationships—Humor. 2. Southern States—
Humor. I. Title: Sissy LeBlanc's rules to live by. II. Title.
　　PS3604.E76 S6 2003
　　813'.6—dc21　　　　　　　　　　　　　　　　2002043246

03 04 05 06 07 ❖/TOP 10 9 8 7 6 5 4 3 2 1

To all those
beautiful Yankees and
their modern Southern sisters
who are intelligent,
well-educated, worked out . . .
and miserable!

Sissy wasn't really beautiful, but men never noticed. With her deep green eyes, her shoulder-length auburn hair that swung when she moved, and the way she moved as if she enjoyed just being inside her body, men had always paid her lots of attention. But then, Sissy thought, it's not what a girl looks like that captivates a man. It's how hard he has to work for her. *A smart girl makes a man sweat.* She decided to make that Rule Number Sixteen in *The Southern Belle's Handbook,* which was what Sissy had ironically titled that compendium of helpful hints and rules her mother and grandmother had tried so hard to instill in her. Her mother had wanted her to grow up a gracious Southern lady. Her grandmother just didn't want the bastards to grind her down. Sissy had added to it over the years, until the Southern Belle's Handbook became her personal credo. She kept it in her head, assigning numbers at random, but then Sissy always had a random relationship with numbers.

—From *The Scandalous Summer of Sissy LeBlanc*

You Don't Have to be Southern

The Southern Belle's Handbook is a survival manual for women. It's a foolproof set of timeless wisdom that can help every woman accomplish exactly what she sets out to achieve in any realm of her life—personal or professional—while avoiding any pitfalls that might stand in her way.

It'll teach you, among other things:

1. How to attract a good man. (It's easy)

2. How to tell if he's good enough for you. (That's harder)

3. How to keep him happy once you've got him. (Piece of cake)

4. How to manage him once you've got him, because even the best men need a little handling. (The easiest of all)

But most important and the most difficult . . .

5. How to take care of yourself, and foster your ambition while radiating a sense of charm and grace.

The Southern Belle's Handbook combines good old-fashioned sense with contemporary courtesy and graciousness. But of course I had to throw in a little sass, because *Life is long and a girl has to have fun while she's still young enough to enjoy it.*

Go ahead, sugar, number that rule yourself.

Sissy
LeBlanc

The Southern Belle's Handbook

It's okay for a woman to know her place,
she just shouldn't stay there.

rule #48

1

You can't change the past, but
a smart girl won't let that stop her.

2

A proper Southern Belle never lets on how bored she is.

rule #77

rule #49

A smart girl can't just sit on the porch and wait for life to start.

4

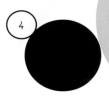

An uppity woman, with enough research,
will find a way.

rule #59

5

 **#1**

What makes you a woman is working up the courage to take your life into your own hands.

The world is lying in wait
to come between a girl and
her ambition.

rule #31

A lady must develop the knack of finding a noble motivation for doing what she wants— or she'll never get a chance to do what she wants at all.

rule #12

rule #51

Life's always harder for a woman. That's why she has to give it a bunch of little shoves and shakes, always taking care the buzzer doesn't ring and the lights don't come on screaming Tilt!

*Don't jump off the roof if you
don't expect to hit the ground.*

*A smart woman never lets
a man know how smart she is.*

rule #28

Any woman who thinks she can get
a man to do anything by going at him
head-on is a fool.

rule #10

Be easy. Let him have his way on little unimportant things. Then when something important to you comes up, you'll be in a position to get what you want without giving up your charm.

rule #38

13

Don't be too easy.
Alpha males love a challenge.
It isn't what you look like
that keeps him on his toes
as much as how hard he
has to work for you. . . .

rule #16

15

A smart girl makes a man sweat.

A Southern Belle picks her fights. . . .

There are so many other ways to get what you want.

rule #26

rule #68

Ask him to do something easy
for you and thank him sweetly.
He'll feel great about himself—
and think you're terrific.

18

A smart girl lets a man take
full credit for doing exactly
what she wants him to do.

When you get to be a certain age you realize that the only thing you have time for is doing exactly what you want.

rule #56

A girl has to look her best
when she's still young enough
to look real good.

rule #64

If you've got it, flaunt it . . .
within reason. Too much
Southern Exposure will
get his attention, but lose
his respect.

22

23

A Southern Belle has to have patience, because a man is often clueless about what he really wants. Of course, after a while patience gets real boring. So if he's too comfortable with "the way things are," a fun-loving Southern Belle has to shake things up.

24

rule #11

Men always find themselves the most fascinating subject of any conversation. When in doubt, let him talk about himself. He'll think you're a brilliant conversationalist.

Everyone likes to feel good about themselves. Especially men. You just kind of help them along. And when they feel good about themselves, they naturally feel good about you.

rule #50

Look at him over your shoulder
or through your eyelashes and
he'll salivate like a Pavlovian dog.
Pat the seat next to you and he'll
come bounding across the room.
It's usually all right to let him sit
on the furniture.

rule #5

Let him know you think he's intelligent and he'll be awed by your perspicacity, even if he can't pronounce the word.

rule #15

Laugh at his wit,
and he'll admire
your sense of humor.

rule #13

29

rule #33

Forget his stomach. The surest way to keep a man happy is to become his cheerleader.

30

rule #73

Men fantasize about being a knight and rescuing a maiden in distress. Encourage this, it's a good thing. There's no reason for you to have to struggle while pushing a heavy bag into an overhead compartment.

*A girl who lets a
boy walk away mad
risks losing him for good.*

rule #8

The best way to get a boy to follow you is to walk out on him. If he's Mr. Right, that's just what he'll do. But some poor misguided men simply aren't able to give you just what you need, much less what you want. The operative word is next!

rule #89

Sometimes doing good
can be delightfully bad.

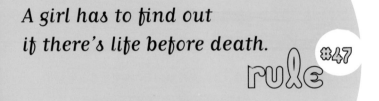

A girl has to find out
if there's life before death.

rule #47

rule **#35**

A woman's greatest power comes not from love, but unrequited lust.

37

Unrequited lust can get real old.

rule #36

rule #42

Love is like cigarettes.
It gives you pleasure while
you're at it, but it sometimes leaves
you with a bad taste in your mouth,
and a pain in your chest.

(39) *A girl doesn't have to give in to temptation but she might not get another chance.*

rule #39

The good Lord wouldn't have made temptations so attractive if He didn't expect us to give in to them every now and then.

rule #34

40

rule #95

A girl can stand just so much virtue.

When deciding whether or not to have sex, a Southern Belle does exactly what she wants while perpetuating the illusion that although this may not be her first time . . .

rule

it's certainly the first time
that ever mattered.

Boys are easy.

A girl has to be honest with herself or she'll never get anything out of life but a palace of lies.

 rule #66

rule #21

A smart girl is picky in her choice of men.

46

Once a girl says yes, it's almost impossible to say no. Boys who respected your wishes before become hard-of-hearing.

rule #9

48

#83

rule

When a man gets hot,
all the blood rushes
from his head, taking
his brain cells along
for the ride.

Men will say anything.
A Southern Belle pays
attention to what he does,
never to what he says.

rule #79

*What men call logic is
all too often a convoluted
rationalization in the service
of their egos, neuroses, and
prejudices. . . .*

rule

Knowing this, a smart woman deals with male "logic" from the vantage point of quiet superiority.

rule #98

Men are fascinated by women.
It's part of Mother Nature's plan.
Any girl can attract a man. Just
take a bath, stand up straight and
send out signals that you're available.

Throughout history, men have drooled over beautiful women. But there's no point obsessing. There are plenty of misguided women who starve themselves to perfection, work out to exhaustion every day, and sit home alone every night—while at the supermarket you'll find lots of women who are fat, fiesty and married. You've got to keep things in perspective.

rule #87

Men are even more insecure than we are. If you can convince yourself you're hot, who are they to disagree? ru£e #85

There are two kinds of men: those who are interested in you and the rest. The second kind are so misguided, they're not worth your time. Because if a man doesn't have the sense to appreciate you, he obviously doesn't have any sense at all.

rule #71

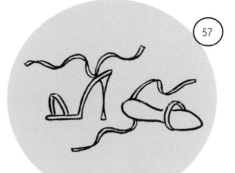

What men find sexy, women find uncomfortable.

rule #45

A man will believe anything as long as it's convenient for him.

Fools and husbands fall for flattery.

rule #18

rule #25

Let a man out of your sight
for a decade and you never
know what he might turn into.

rule #94

No matter how much you love them, beware of other people's plans for your own good.

61

A lady shouldn't have to fight
to get what she wants.

rule #20

rule #102

Don't ditch a girlfriend for a mere date. Boyfriends may come and go, but a girlfriend is forever.

83

rule #100

Letting go is the best revenge.
It frees your heart for much
more satisfying pursuits.

rule #70

If you want to "abstain from fleshly lusts, which war against the soul," just marry him.

rule #55

So much of the unpleasantness in a marriage is a direct result of the husband feeling underappreciated.

Never marry a man who makes your skin crawl.

rule #57

rule #43

Don't settle for a man
too stupid for you.
He'll spend the rest of
your life getting even.

68

69

You can't hold on to
a dead relationship,
but remember what
Ralph Waldo Emerson
said: "When half-gods
go / The gods arrive."

rule #103

rule #54

A woman who goes out with a married man plays second fiddle to his wife—Southern Belles don't make that kind of music.

70

(71)

Whatever happens, they always blame the girl.

rule #6

When caught red-handed,
lie through your teeth.

rule #3

Never leave any man you are even slightly interested in alone with the Other Woman.

rule #30

A lady doesn't waste her time on bad memories.

rule

74

rule #23

When a train heads straight at you, a smart girl derails it.

The best defense is often a diversion.

rule #14

76

rule **#29**

When a lady's actions
are not beyond reproach
she never refers to them.

The Southern Belle's Handbook

Below is space to make note of your own Rules for Life.

_____

_____

_____

_____

_____

_____

_____

_____